CLASSIC PICTURE BOOKS OF YUNNAN ETHNIC GROUPS

The Origin of the City of Dawn

By Sunshine Orange Studio

Translated by Zhao Mingzhen

Adapted by Joe Gregory

Books Beyond Boundaries

ROYAL COLLINS

The Origin of the City of Dawn

By Sunshine Orange Studio
Translated by Zhao Mingzhen
Adapted by Joe Gregory

First published in 2022 by Royal Collins Publishing Group Inc.
Groupe Publication Royal Collins Inc.
BKM Royalcollins Publishers Private Limited

Headquarters: 550-555 boul. René-Lévesque O Montréal (Québec) H2Z1B1 Canada
India office: 805 Hemkunt House, 8th Floor, Rajendra Place, New Delhi 110 008

Original Edition © Yunnan Education Publishing House Co., Ltd.

ISBN: 978-1-4878-1016-0

To find out more about our publications, please visit www.royalcollins.com.

Once upon a time, the city of Jinghong was called "Mengle." Long before any humans had come to the fertile land near the Lancang River, you could hear the birds and smell the fragrance of flowers. Many rare birds and animals lived freely and happily in Mengle.

Not far away from this paradise was a place called Mengzhanbanaguan (today called Menghun), where a tribe of the Dai people lived. The head of the tribe was a talented young man named Payalawu.

After Payalawu became the head of Mengzhanbanaguan, he often led young men hunting in the forests in order to get enough food and warm clothes for the people. Each and every time they went out, they would come back with their hands full. Then Payalawu would divide their bounty with the people according to what they had killed, while also making sure that it was evenly divided between the people who had stayed at home. Therefore, he was deeply loved by his tribe.

But one year, the mountain forests around Mengzhanbanaguan were destroyed in a big forest fire and the animals all died or ran away. Even though Payalawu had great abilities, he was unable to find enough food for the tribe.

Under great hardship and suffering, the tribe made it through to the next spring. When Payalawu saw the tender little shoots of grass emerging on the bare, fire-burnt hillside near the tribe, he thought to himself, "Spring is coming. Everything is coming back to life. Should I lead our people to go hunting in a distant forest? There should be animals in the forest that we can hunt."

Early that morning, Payalawu beat the big drum used to summon the people to discuss important tribal issues. He announced that he had decided to go hunting in the mountains far away. He said, "I'm going to try my luck in the far mountains. Would you like to go with me?"

The oldest man in the tribe stepped out of the crowd, bowed with his palms together, and expressed the will of all, "Honorable Zhaomeng (the chief of a Dai tribe), we are all your faithful people. The old men, like me, cannot ride a horse or pull a bow. We will stay here to guard the village. All the others will follow you."

Payalawu was delighted to see that everyone was willing to follow him. He held his palms together and bowed to the senior man and the people.

Finally a day for the journey was chosen and Payalawu led the hunting expedition in the direction of Mengle.

They crossed rivers, went through thick forests, and climbed high mountains. On the way, they saw birds in the sky, but saw no animals on the ground. They were only able to get a few pheasants every day.

Payalawu was very frustrated and disappointed. He decided not to lead his people any further on this adventure, and that they would return to Mengzhanbanaguan after one night's rest.

The next morning, Payalawu gathered everyone. His heart was heavy, seeing his people's tired but trusting faces. Apologetically, he said to everyone, "Since we left home, we haven't gotten enough game to eat, nor have we slept well. For our safety, we have to go back."

But just as they had packed up and were ready to return, a golden deer leaped out of the woods, galloping towards them and stopping at a hillside not far from Payalawu.

The golden deer was strong and beautiful,
with a golden halo shining over its head.

What the people did not know was that this magical golden deer was the embodiment of the goddess Payaying. She wanted to bring Payalawu and his people to Mengle, a land with fertile soil and much water and grass, where the people could live happily and raise their children in peace and quiet.

In trying to recover from the surprise of seeing a golden deer, Payalawu drew his bow and arrow and fired at it. The arrow struck the hind leg of the golden deer. But when Payalawu walked towards the golden deer, it galloped away unharmed.

Payalawu hurriedly commanded his hunting team to go with him after the golden deer. The deer would run for a bit, and then stop, just to start running again as the people got closer. The deer's strange behavior awoke Payalawu and his hunting team's fighting spirit.

After continuously chasing the deer, they arrived at a valley called Jilawai, which was full of wisteria. Some of the men could not run anymore, so they asked for a rest.

They kept chasing the golden deer, although they all felt tired. If some were tired and sick, other people would help them. Some rode on elephants and horses, or were even carried by their companions. Seeing the people helping their comrades moved Payalawu to tears. He let the sick people stay to recover. Leaving food and water and a man to take good care of them, Payalawu then led the rest of his team to chase the golden deer.

Closely following the pace of the golden deer, Payalawu and his people crossed mountains and passed through lush forests. The golden deer seemed to know when the people were tired. She often stopped to let Payalawu and his team take a break.

Finally, Payalawu led the people out of the deep forests and into Mengle, the goddess Payaying's intended destination all along. Payalawu could see how the golden deer stopped right in front of him. With a flash of golden light, the golden deer disappeared.

Dawn was approaching and the sun rose in the east.

The people were tired, supporting each other as they walked out of the deep forest. Before them, a large flat land of flowers, grass, and rich soil appeared.

Payalawu was very excited when he saw this flat land. The climate was warm and humid, and the vast land was fertile; it was much better suited for people than Mengzhanbanaguan. Immediately, they fell in love with the land.

Payalawu decided that this would be their new home. He sent people to get those who stayed in Mengzhanbanaguan and those who were left along the way. They started building up a city and gradually, more and more people came to settle down in the newfound place.

After they arrived at their new home at dawn, Payalawu named this paradise "Jinghong," which in the Dai language means "City of Dawn."